Noble Orphan

Noble Orphan

poems by Andrea Nicki

Demeter Press, Bradford, Ontario

Published by:
Demeter Press
140 Holland Street West
P. O. Box 13022
Bradford, ON L3Z 2Y5
Tel: (905) 775-9089
Email: info@demeterpress.org
Website: www.demeterpress.org

Demeter Press logo based on Skulptur "Demeter" by Maria-Luise Bodirsky <www.keramik-atelier.bodirsky.edu>

Cover Artwork: Julie Hammond of Iris Artworks, "Soeur Béatrice," Detail, 1996; 2012, sanded latex and oil paint on drywall, 11.72" x 21.063"

Printed and Bound in Canada

Library and Archives Canada Cataloguing in Publication
        Noble orphan / Andrea Nicki

ISBN 978-1-927335-11-6

Cataloguing data available from Library and Archives Canada.

To my feminist mentors

ALSO BY ANDREA NICKI

Welcoming

Contents

Homeless Neighbour

Noble Orphan

Sufi Heat Rose

Preface

I wrote these poems between 2007-2010. From 2007-2009, I worked as an instructor of ESL for a class of immigrant women in Vancouver. I was inspired by the courage and endurance of the women seeking a better life for their children and learning a difficult new language. Several of them had worked as professionals in their countries of origin and were raising their children alone while their husbands continued to work abroad as the financial providers.

Teaching ESL to immigrants isn't simply a matter of teaching the mechanics and content of a language, but also about a new culture and its ways. Canadian culture is diverse, with clashing ideologies, and ESL teachers unavoidably impart their own sets of values and ideals. In my case I promoted care and community.

Although I was their teacher and host I often found myself on the receiving end of hospitality, as some of the women enjoyed sharing their cultures with me and having me over for ethnic meals. These women later engaged me as a private tutor for their children. The children struggled hard in their new schools with unfamiliar systems and I was impressed by their strengths of character, creativity, and independent thought. Not having children of my own to look after, in several instances I went beyond my duties as a tutor and engaged in mothering. Sometimes my cross-cultural mothering could be difficult and demoralizing because of a conflict in values with immigrant mothers and challenges that they were facing.

My experience with cross-cultural mothering led me to reflect more on a variety of related topics and issues: traditional mothering and fathering; the social constructions of masculinity and femininity; violence in gender relations; child abuse and the lack of communal responsibility for child welfare; home and homelessness; mental health and psychiatry; trauma and healing; female friendship and community; ecofeminist spirituality; and animal and environmental protection. The title, *Noble Orphan*, alludes to different forms of neglect and abuse children can suffer in societies where child needs are not treated as vitally important, and children's oppression is supported by interlocking systems of oppression. Like my first poetry book *Welcoming* (Inanna Publications), *Noble Orphan* challenges destructive values while promoting ecofeminist ones, a cooperative, ecologically sustainable world with "beehive love" (from "Beehive Love").

Teaching ESL

Sea Accent

I have tuned my voice
to the sounds of the sea
my accent is difficult
to practice listening
bring a large seashell
close to your ear

Pronunciation

Chinese woman struggles hard
to make F and P sounds
fun pain pale puffy panting puffing...
her mouth going strong and stronger
for Olympic gold
fast famous face

Crescent Moon

I teach *crescent* avenue
area of close, loving neighbours
crescent moon smiling brightly
with open homes, potlucks
and carpools

Teaching ESL

1.

I give them listening exercises with John Denver
Simon & Garfunkel, the Beatles
A woman understands well my point
says, "I think Canadian women like men
who are kind and peaceful"

2.

I teach them about Canadian geography
North American dating, falling in love:
"Two people meet at Niagara Falls
and fall in love, jump into the rapids"

Yellow Plastic Case

Chinese lawyer
with yellow plastic case
full of exercise books
learning survival English
hour after hour repeating words:
apple, banana, orange ...
while her child does the same

Chinese Mothers

1.

We will learn English
and help our children in their education
but we will learn it our way:
no oversweet donuts or caramelized apples
for their tongues
no oversexualization of our bodies
no medicalization of our moon time
no disrespect of mothers

2.

I keep their warm smiles close
to my baby steps
as I sound my first Mandarin words
my eyes narrowing with Chinese joy

Chang'e

The Chinese women
reminisce about the moon festival
and how they celebrate it:
eating moon cake on their balconies
looking at Chang'e in the sky

make luminous sentences
walk   around   each   ~~words~~ word
~~on~~ in their   moon   mist
pick one up and keep it
or let it sink back into the earth

*The Chinese Moon Festival is on the fifteenth day of the eighth lunar month and is full of ancient legends, such as the legend of the emperor Houyi and the moon goddess Chang'e. Many Chinese people set up outdoor altars facing the moon to worship her and receive her blessing.

Chinese Friend

1.

A Chinese woman tells me there is a saying in Chinese about what to do
when your husband is looking for a second wife:
"Keep one eye open and the other one closed"
I meet her husband who is very complimentary
She looks at me, one eye open, the other one closed

2.

Language Reference: Adjective Order

Opinion + Age + Pattern, Colour + Material + Style + Noun

wonderful middle-aged professional Chinese immigrant friend

Beehive Love

At the class party
women from around the world
dance hand-in-hand
or with arms loosely around waists
"Lesbian"? Close, but not quite
a matriarchal lovely thing ...
what is the word? *Beehive love*

Teaching Children

Did you *laugh*
when you got out
of your mother's belly
or did you *cry?*

Did you *swim*
in your mother's belly
or only *float?*

Young Sappho

Thirteen-year-old girl
came to Canada two years ago
one-child family
first-generation immigrant
her parents' hopes, dreams, future
private ESL lessons three times a week
Her mother tells her she must
work hard to go to university
and make the family proud
marry well and give them grandchildren
"*Every* day she tells me," the girl complains
We are learning the expression
to have faith in
"Who do you have faith in?" I ask
I look around the basement apartment
spotting a wooden cross on the wall
"I have faith in my mother," she responds
"No, not really."   Her eyes tighten
"I have faith in myself," she says
fuchsia rising in her cheeks
"I think I am a lesbian"

Fifteen-Year-Old Girl

I tell the fifteen-year-old girl
about an old English custom
involving romance
between a boy and girl:
a heart carved with a knife
on a tree, two names etched inside

I write on a piece of paper:

> Jill Green + Jack Smith

then tell Jill dreams
of becoming Mrs. Smith

"It's not fair!" she shouts
and rips the couple in two

Young Nature Goddess

Six-year-old girl
has a pet ladybug
for half-an-hour
She puts it in
a small glass jar
with bits of green leaves
draws a picture of it
and a girl
with a ladybug-pendant
around her neck
then lets the tiny creature go

Rectangle

New immigrant
in English mathematics
doesn't know the word for rectangle
doesn't want to ask the teacher—
what will the other students think?
people learn words for shapes in preschool
"Qing, Qing, what is the answer?"
the teacher asks
The problem looks very familiar
she has done hundreds like these
and ones much easier
"But what part is *rectangle*?"
she thinks to herself
The other new immigrants
at her rectangular table
look at her in support
"Okay, someone else?" the teacher says

Father

Father angry because he wants
his son's English writing
to be spectacular

four paragraphs
each with its own special energy
like four planets aligned powerfully in the sky

Airplane

Student angry about her father
going back to China for three more months
stares at the photograph
of her family on her keychain
touches her father
uses a picture of him
as her computer's screen saver
kneeling with his arms spread out

Pink Girl

1.

It's Valentine's Day
I'm teaching a girl
who loves cute things
and anything with hearts
At age 10 she is a wisp of a tree
two plastic daisies looping her fingers
her clothes fashionable and pink
silver sparkles on her cheeks

Talking about music lessons, dance lessons
her smile outshines Shirley Temple's
If you didn't really know her
you would think she was spoiled
and you would think she would be especially happy today
from handing out cards to all her classmates
and being surrounded by admirers

I ask her whether there was a party at school
She answers quickly, then scowls and shows me
a picture story book called "Angry Girl"
she drew and wrote herself in sharp-pointed pencil
She hates a girl at school who has been bullying her

says she fought so much with her that
her "fire hit the sky":
"the bad yesterday was much better than today"

2.

The next day she says proudly
she is wearing a new sweater
from her "friend-enemy"
I tell her about the time a girl told me
every day at school that she hated me
"Why?" she asks. "No reason," I answer
"Maybe she was jealous about something"
"What does jealous mean?" she asks
I give her the definition
"I don't feel jealous," she says
"I love everyone. I am an angel"
trying to fly away from our lesson

3.

I'm trying to teach the pink girl
the use of the colon
I tell her if I open my fridge door
I will see five things:
a bottle of soya milk
a bag of carrots
a left-over potato
a carton of free-range eggs
and a container of yogurt

I ask "What will you see
if you open your fridge door?"
She looks thoughtful
about to produce, I think
a list of her own wholesome items
copying the teacher
instead she says
"I see a leg, an arm, an eyeball
bloody hair, an ear"
"My, my," I say steadily, but feeling uncomfortable
"It seems like someone has been watching
some scary movies"
I try to redirect her attention
back to wholesome things:
"What would you see in your fridge
right now?"
But she gives more macabre details
presents more body parts

One-Year-Old Girl

One-year-old girl gives me her face for a kiss
is starting to learn love
I give her the light touch of the dragonfly
so she will learn the right kind

Young Nature God

Seven-year-old boy
loves the whole of nature
even the legs of a spindly spider
do not escape his notice and care
When he accidentally stepped on some
he apologized to the spider
it died so he gave it a blessing
scraping it carefully off the ground
so that each infinitesimal part
would not go to waste
then placed it next to a feeding bee

Saint Halloween

Chinese immigrant
her first time trick-or-treating
gets a lot of candy
Her older sister rushes out, looks in her bag
snatches chocolate bars
handing me some
I go to see the little girl's face
expecting an angry jack o' lantern
instead she dumps the rest of her treats
into the two large bowls
her mother has prepared for visitors
The doorbell rings
She gives out the rest of the candy
in large handfuls to children
going back and forth
until everything is gone

Private Tutor

1.

She has returned home
my private student
who I have loved as my own
nurtured, counselled
helped with difficult situations
her mother away night after night
I go to her house
it's her mother's birthday
She says her mother needs help
with an English name
for their new baby sister
her voice is sharp, insistent
She hasn't done any of her homework
or read any of the books we spent
over two hours looking for
I ask her what she did on her vacation
She talks about going with her father
and just watching him work at his hotels
and drink alcohol
She wanted to come home
but her mother wouldn't allow it

2.

Birthday party hats, noise makers, balloons
my student anxious
at her mother's side
my student, not my niece
or even my distant cousin

in my head a large balloon deflating

Mother's Day

Pink carnations for the mothers?
Am I not a mother too? doing motherwork
caring for children as *my* children

I close my eyes and imagine some flowers
with otherworldly colors and intensity
falling into my arms

Worker Bee

1.

Think like a worker bee
think of the whole

"Slumming in this ESL school?"
a co-worker who knows
I have a doctorate
says to me
Do bees ever *slum*?

2.

Language reference: new idioms

New Idiom	Meaning	Example
To not fit in	To be different from a group of people; to not belong	You are over-qualified and don't fit in here. Your skills are too high for immigrants.
To be let go	To lose your job	She was let go and told to return the key to the front door.

Homeless Neighbour

homeless neighbour

sixteen-year-old girl
sitting on the pavement
her cardboard sign
heavy with snow
fallen on her lap
like a collapsed roof

Stee-people

At a church thrift sale:

"That will be $20 for the 10 pairs"
A church member replies: "But I only have $10
I want to buy all of these shoes
to send to relatives in Peru"
"$2 for each pair. Sorry, no deals
We need to raise $3000 for our church
to renovate our stee-people"

Animal Bite

A friend tells me about a nasty animal bite
The dog was put to sleep
She wonders still if she should sue the owner
I tell her about a human bite
a venomous person in the office
almost sending me into anaphylactic shock
The person is still there, I tell her
Just a personality conflict the manager said

Synchronicity

I talk to the wrong poet
he treats me like a high school student
a young female fan
I go to the wrong movie
a movie about a "she-devil"
leave before the grand seduction scene
A skunk and I are in synchronicity
It runs across the street under a car
is nearly hit, moves just in time
returns to its garden
My bus is late and it is dark
a Rolls-Royce pulls up
an old gentleman with his son and
"partner," this welcoming word
offers me a lift
invites me to talk about myself
my plans, my woman writer plans
the skunk and I safe back to our homes

99 Express Bus

On an overcrowded 99 express bus
passengers far over the red line
the driver talks on his cellphone
to a crisis line worker about his life
says he is tired of the pain

Endangered

Do endangered species
have suicidal thoughts?
experience near extinction
or simply exist?

Some endangered species
disguise themselves like butterflies
use cryptic coloration
have adapted their colours
over generations
so that they blend in with
dull, bureaucratic environments

Radio Broadcaster

A radio broadcaster talks about
environmental threats to bees
and some bees separated from their hive
living out their last days in her house's eaves
Her response: "Maybe they should try Facebook"

pilgrimage to burns bog

1.

environmentalist
passionate about a bog
greener than green
fluorescent green
like a red-eyed tree frog

2.

downed tree
her branches curved
like a ribcage

3.

tree had let her bark fall just so
made a heart shape
for us to see
so we would love her

4.

long mossy branches
hanging low like furry
snuffleupagus noses
waving hello

*Burns Bog is the largest peat bog on the west coast of North America and is situated in
southeastern British Columbia.
*A snuffleupagus is a furry, elephant-like mammal in the TV series Sesame Street. Some
snuffleupaguses are a mossy green colour.

River

The river carries
a piece of paper
a bottle, a plastic bag
swallows human debris
with stained, oily lips

left-over dinner
in a stryrofoam box
tossed with resentment
by a man
who thought he would
do better than this
find a wife and become rich

His kiss always slips
as the water keeps moving

Siamese Cat

I have been trying to show my cat
the same amount of high respect
as was shown to her ancestors of Siam
restricted to royal families and served on golden plates
Having comparatively meagre means I do my best
buying her lots of toys: soft crinkly balls, catnip pillows
sticks with hanging feathers

She likes to go out but we live near busy traffic
so I take her out on a long leash
Her favourite bird to hunt is the crow
perhaps tapping into genetic memories
of more formidable distant ancestors
who would have had a much better chance at catching one
than my cat with her dainty, tentative paws

Her favourite toy is a stick with pink feathers
which I wave while she jumps and swats at it
She likes to hide under the dresser
and watch the feathers as they move across the floor
She understands that "zigzag bird"
is just a game, that I'm the one making the feathers
fly, soar, drop in altitude, circle, land
disappear behind a hedge of blanket

a tree-door
and that the feathers in her mouth are not a dead crow
She often plays with this feather-toy by herself
making it rise and fall

Amazed and admiring that she can derive so much enjoyment
from this poor facsimile of the natural world
I try to copy her, imagine that I too am in a world
that does not fall short of a rich ideal
where limitations can be magically transformed
consolations affording great delight

Feline Love

My cat is very sociable
she likes to be close to the neighbouring cat
and sits outside his door for hours
making sweet sound
listening to his bell tinkle just inches away
his paws scratching futilely to get out
We never hear him speak
he is a quiet fellow, but I don't think
his voice would be filled with
coloratura song of doomed love
Felines know nothing of this
having many playmates is best, they teach us

Trouba's Kitten Book

June 1, 2010

New big bushy cats next door
Trouba's first hiss

June 4, 2010

We play "chase"
My red-haired friend is Ginger Cat
I am Honey Cat
Trouba is Trouba

June 6, 2010

Powerful wind
tries to lift Trouba
off the ground
like Toto
in *The Wizard of Oz*
being pulled up
by a tornado

*The name "Trouba" is from the word "troubairitz." The troubairitz were French female poet-composers of the twelvth and thirteenth centuries who wrote secular music about courtly love and their romantic desires and frustrations.

to my less furr-urr-y friends

haven't been writing purr poems
because urr have been having
mee-ow hands furry full with fost-urr-ing
two purr purrfect kittens
and purrlaying with them
and losing mee-ow command
of urr human lang-urr-ge

Noble Orphan

Hospital Birth Record

I took my first breath on September 29, 1969
My cry was "strong" for five days
What was my mother thinking? feeling?
The record only mentions the condition
of her genitals—"swollen"
that she was breast-feeding me
that the umbilical cord had healed

Where was my father? His thoughts? Feelings?
What about my older sister?
Was she at my mother's bedside in love with me?

Astrological Natal Chart

1.

I was born on September 29, 1969
at 2:20 a.m.
while five planets in the third house
started their music, their slow churning inside

2.

Heavy Libran influence

yoke worn over the neck of an ox
human head and arms secured
as in Medieval stocks
beast of burden, martyr

*In astrology the third house is the house of relationships. A heavy Libran with a lot of
planets in her/his third house would likely be, according to professional astrologers, very
preoccupied with balance in relationships and society.*

Alignment

I'm trying to align myself properly
I'm three-quarters of the way there
but to be honest
my neck is still a bit twisted
and I'm still looking the wrong way

A very serious near-fatal injury
caused by familial abuse
neglectful neighbours
a communal failure to intercede
crude medicine that can't sense
the soul in its contortions
trying to measure it with solid instruments
analyzing samples of tissue and blood

Anti-Hopscotches

One needle mark scar on my left arm
from extractions of blood after trauma and collapse
one single needle print is not much
I never thought I would make it this far to the age of 38
never imagined me here alive
thought only of the next year at best
The fifteen-year-old girl on the street corner downtown
who is thinking only of her next hour
so many criss-crosses, anti-hopscotches

Mood Lenses

Is it better with this or *this?*
the doctor asks, fitting her
Seroquel + Effexor + Ativan
or Seroquel + Trazodone
This or *this?*
Seroquel + Effexor + Ativan + Trazodone
or Effexor + Zyprexa?

*These names refer to pharmaceuticals prescribed for severe-to-moderate depression and anxiety.

Psychiatric Protocol

Patient reports suicidal ideation.

How often does the patient think of suicide?

1.   If every day, go to question 2.

2.   Does the patient have a suicide plan? If no, go to question
3. Test for personality disorder.

3.   Does the patient exhibit impulsive behaviour, such as
spending large sums of money? If patient says no, continue with
other questions. Patient must have at least # _ of symptoms in order
to be diagnosed as having a personality disorder.

4.   Ask patient about sexual orientation. Is the patient some-
times confused about this?

Doctor writes: Patient says no, but is upset about this question.
Complains about being compulsively drawn to bad situations "like
a broken compass." Unclear.

5.   Does the patient fear abandonment?

Doctor writes: Patient starts to cry. I repeat the question. Patient is very angry. Says family abandoned her. Glares and stops talking, says doesn't like being tested for a personality disorder, doesn't believe in personality disorders, finds them "demeaning and disrespectful." Patient very uncooperative and angry. Borderline personality disorder.

Foot Poems

1.

My left foot hurts when I walk
I have worn out the plantar fascia
from walking too long and too far
It wants to rest somewhere
and not have to move
I curve my foot around a nest's egg
and try to lift it

2.

The doctor tells me I don't
walk properly
my feet positioning to go up
a mountain every time

She wraps my left foot in white tape
but this is too flimsy for others
to write encouraging messages on

3.

My feet have to let go and keep
stepping away
away from narcissists
away from users and their supporters
away from abusive lovers
away from egotistical peers

4.

Difficult steps into a new world
it's hard to see where I'm stepping
the earth is bright and then black

Grey Mood

1.

In a grey mood on Easter Sunday
all I see is the long grey street
with bumps and potholes
as I ride down it on my bike
not needing to pedal
not needing any movement or action
trees, houses pass
fall away as flat as stage sets

I cry but it's like I'm someone
in a picture crying
and there's no one to reach me

It's sunny today
blue sky appears between branches
but as if someone coloured it in
with a paint brush

2.

My landlord is angry
I have locked my keys inside
my apartment
says I have taken him away
from a family gathering
enjoying the sunny weather
My tearing eyes respond
at least you have a family

Co-dependent Marriage

Vowing to be each other's
moon, sun, stars, ocean, lake
pond, mud puddle, rock, seashell
pebble, gravel, particle of dirt

Moths

1.

Over thirty moths in my kitchen
three cocoons all in a row
sealed between the wall and ceiling
like three separate rooms in a moth hotel
I call my landlord for help
his face at the door
worrying aloud about his property
the stains on the walls
not caring about my grey shaking hands

2.

I ignore a few grains on the kitchen table
and let some moths fly at liberty
in the living room
co-dependent love
or overextended generosity
in a world of home ownership?

Blue Eyes

1.

A black woman says
to an anorexic blond woman:
You're like a real Barbie
I want your blue eyes
You're so lucky to have those eyes
big and blue, those are the best kind

I want to take them out
and twist and screw them
into my eye sockets

Blue eyes would have protected me
from all this pain
my boyfriend wouldn't have left me
I would have a better job
I would be rich and happy

2.

The anorexic blond woman has
no stomach, a clothes-hanger back
bony arms hanging like canes
a nose too large for her teaspoon-shaped face

She is married to Ken but he has affairs
She had a high-paying job
but was always fighting with her staff
and got sick and had to stop working
Her parents are not the supportive kind—
(who has ever heard of Barbie's parents?)
She is estranged from Junior Barbie who is a lesbian
She has been diagnosed with a mystery illness
and is leaving the country in search of a cure
The search to solve a complicated puzzle, her father told her
"Keep us posted on your search" he said
"on your speedy recovery"   recovery like a missile
her blue eyes not blue enough
a blue blindfold

*This poem is partially a response to Toni Morrison's novel, The Bluest Eye, about
an economically poor black girl who is raped by her father. She believes, based on the
images of happy, blond, blue-eyed children that surround her, that if she had "the bluest
eyes" these would protect her from her father's violence and transform her life, and looks
for someone to magically give her them.

Cousins

1.

Her cousin tells her his life story
surviving hits at home
talks about his problem with drugs
heroin, his dealing of heroin
his problem with sex, the rape of his ex-wife
She tells him about sexual trauma, brain injury
desertion of relatives, exile

2.

He wraps a bandage around her head
She dresses his broken nose
They lie close to each other on the grass
like two children
talking about their fathers
and brutal childhoods

3.

He tells her things heavily, shockingly
not really taking much care
his own bitterness absorbing him
and then more helpfully

validates her pain, her experience
He says they are near-twins:
We are the black sheep
We are the outcasts
We are the orphaned
We are part of the whole story
about two other orphans—two brothers, their fathers
and their own brutal childhoods

4.

Her cousin is violent
she is self-destructive
victimizervictim they are, a messy organism
a stinging jellyfish

Meanwhile the newspapers and academic articles
talk about sex offenders and what to do about them
how to stop them and whether they should be castrated
and about incest victims and how to treat them
their personality disorders and suicide rates

What about this jellyfish, then, washed up on the shore
innocently sitting there?

~~Father-Daughter Incest ?~~
~~Father-Daughter Relationship ?~~

Father Sex Crimes

Listening to a woman's account
of father sex crimes
I keep seeing layers and layers
of hands all over her body
images that have lingered, accumulated
from unpunished assaults
That there are two separate things
is very clear: his hands and her body
not a shared hideousness, a shared gene
not her "partially genetic personality disorder"
his ruinous crimes, *his* shameful secrets, *his* blight
his daughter so enamoured of her father, her provider
just as any child is taught
a daisy turned toward the sun-god
This isn't a love story gone wrong
all her petals torn off, stripped tragically
to "he loves her not"
This is a child's reasonable expectation
that her father
isn't her own private
Paul Bernardo

Paul Bernardo is a convicted Canadian serial killer and rapist who committed his crimes in the 1980's. His father was charged with sexually molesting a girl, and sexually abused his daughter, Bernardo's sister.

Fire-Eater

A father's treachery
my rage is so strong
my words catch on fire

hurricane thomas: a traumatic re-enactment

1.

the new lovers are sky divers
flying in the wind
they are children spinning
on the merry-go-round
they are a black squirrel and grey
squirrel chasing each other
they are two crows with beaks parted open

2.

their bold spirits tweak the lgbttqq rainbow
with their own colours
she starts to feel better
but is it oxygen or chloroform?

3.

she slides her fingers through
his brown chest hair
soft and ropy—like a fisherman's net?

4.

v-brain food   ∨∨∨∨∨//
∨∨∨∨∨∨∨∨∨∨∨∨∨∨∨∨∨∨∨∨∨∨∨∨∨/
    brain stimulation brain massage brain-licking
    brain-rubbing of damaged hypothalamus
          turning red into pink
          pink brain waves
        pink-yellow brain waves
        brain rapture orgasm
          ∨∨∨//
            ∨ /

5.

these lips of hers...like a loose begonia or rose?
his tongue long inside tells her differently
seeking its own rapture its own aphrodisiac
these lips the opening of a new world
        \ /

6.

finger rubbing stirring pink mouth pink lips
pink tongue pink feelings pink thoughts
pink pleasure pink touches pink kisses
pink love pink vagina pink vagina juice
pink river pink ocean pink time travel pink galaxy
pink universe

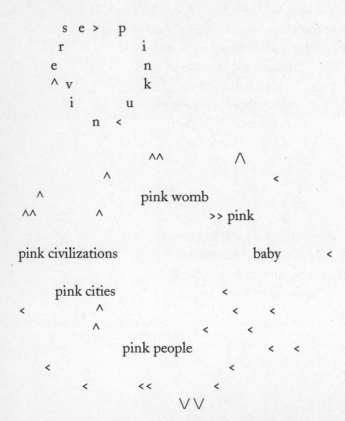

```
      s  e  >    p
       r             i
      e             n
     ^ v            k
       i          u
         n   <
```

pink womb

>> pink

pink civilizations   baby   <

        pink cities   <

pink people

VV

7.

the man is like a little boy out on the beach
who sees something strange in the sand
maybe a treasure
he bends down, gets closer and closer
wanting to pick it up
but fearing it might be something terrible
a claw, a huge wild bird pulling him
through sand to some prehistoric world

8.

the man imagines fangs
with a sharp, nasty bite
a pornographic she-devil
later his tongue inside her again
a little more relaxed
but afraid of molars

ancient stones laid down thousands
of years ago
part of an ancient pagan village
afraid of the deep, deep flower of her
an exotic whorl, a time warp

9.

red man red anger red insults
memories of red father red alcoholic eyes

red spankings red wallops with a belt
red burns red sores red mosquito bites
red boiling water red hits

red anger red man red snarling red yapping biting
red situation red unsafety red terror red air
red chest red man shaking red shouts

10.

the man wanting more pink aphrodisiac
craving pink aphrodisiac he is so scared inside
great trembling tremors shaking earthquake thundering storm
wrecking hurricane hurricane thomas
yelling in the storm slashing trashing

11.

the calm woman can get to safety
she can get to friends pick up the phone and call talk listen
talk listen hug shake hands for bravery

12.

the red man thrashing crashing

13.

the woman can compose her thoughts

14.

the red man's thoughts too tight no air
despair gloom anomie paranoia chaos avalanches

15.

no enticing smell comes from his sex
no whiff at all no erotic appeal
a man who hates his own feminine side
hatred for the woman's smaller fingers and nails
for her joys from "little" things, love for children
for her "ten-year-old" energy
hatred for her "malicious jealousy"
for her desire for monogamy and specialness
a "childish" desire, he says
hatred for spontaneity

16.

this man with his porno-woman-loving-woman-hating
odorless sex watery aphrodisiac

17.

this man with his porno-woman-loving-woman-hating
comparing competing fighting arguing
desexualizing desexing asexual plant

18.

the woman rejoins friends children playing

19.

the man red ball in his face red ball in his face
every muscle tendon fibre aching paining
nerve vein cell exploding bleeding out slithering excreting

20.

the woman painting writing poeming
adopting befriending single mothers children
"schizophrenics" people with "asperger's"

21.

red man picking at red skin biting himself tasting his blood
mixing it with ketchup hot sauce

22.

the woman shares raspberries strawberries fruit punch
pink lemonade rhubarb pie

23.

the treasure wanting to be picked up
by the interested curious man

wanting to be loved explored

the man's clumsy touch
narrowness of vision undersight oversight

the curtains quickly pulled down from the sky
the clouds the darkness pulled
snuffing out all the stars
there is no peep show for you, mr. thomas

Vagina Dentata

There was a time when women
actually had these teeth
an evolutionary adaptation of female warriors
not just a morbid fantasy, a myth

Somehow the teeth started to fall out
stopped growing in newborn girgoyles
but people feared they might return

and then what was spread to stop their re-emergence
keep women flaccid and slow to revolt?
a story about a woman deeply interested in teeth
but not for herself, not for her own needs and safety—
The Tooth Fairy—
giving children money for useless teeth
disposing of them discretely
out of the kindness of her heart
performing a thankless and exhausting task
of visits to thousands of children every night
all the time gentle and benign
her arms never tugging forcefully at a pillow
and knocking a child in the head
wanting no return or reward
not even a child's dozy smile, an iron bust in her honor

I tell you now, children and adults
there is no such thing as the Tooth Fairy
but there is the Tooth Witch
Wherever you may have disposed of teeth
she will find them
and use them in a potent brew
with motherwort leaves, deer antler, watermelon seeds
in a spiritual invocation to make the warrior teeth
come back, back to the ancient sheath

*"Sheath" has a double meaning; it refers to both a vagina and a case for a sword. This poem was inspired by the movie, Teeth, written and directed by Mitchell Lichtenstein.

prayer for incest survivors

o goddess o sacred circle o mother of motherless o sister of sisterless
o brother of brotherless o father of fatherless o family of familyless
o city of cityless o country of countryless o world of worldless o

rage

after a volcano erupts
grey ash forms curvy clouds
a mystical paisley pattern

rage can be directed into
a sacred form

red dragonfly

make your anger flit lightly
like a red dragonfly
propelled by transparency
sensitive but able to see an object
from many different sides
in many different lights
and change direction easily
going backwards if needed
to see what was missed

Matron Saint of Valentine's Day

At a support group for incest survivors
a woman talks about crime after crime
without any emotion
I think her heart should have stopped
from the surfeit of human evil
How can she be living? I wonder
especially on Valentine's Day
a day so dependent on the human heart
Something else is keeping her alive
a vision of repeated victimization
transcended in collective action
She presents us each with a pink teddy bear
rising above the expected

Twins

We complain about the mess of our lives
I look up to see the mess of the sky
instead a pink sunset splitting perfectly

Noble Orphan

The person who leaves
an unlivable family
and sets off on a difficult course
far from being a family traitor
is the one who in the end
preserves the good family name
and the honour of more noble ancestors
who knew how to love children properly
sustain a full family tree

On Reviving Socrates

We could invent some technology
that could undo his death, revitalize ancient cells from the dust
and encourage him to couple with a modern day Hypatia
We could find genes associated with philosophical thinking
engineer multiple embryos and use preimplantation genetic
  diagnosis to ensure
Hypatia gives birth to philosophical octuplets
Hypatia was by all accounts not only a great philosopher
but also a great mathematician and astronomer
Further, she was known for her virtue and feminist boldness
We could select genes associated with mathematical ability
scientific analysis, virtue, and feminist boldness, and engineer variety
Socrates was also a great teacher and mentor of youth
We could select genes associated with these skills
There could be diverse philosophical offspring that could deepen
  different areas of public life
Finally, we could construct a new illness: "critical thinking
  deficit disorder"
and ensure all those suffering get free pharmaceuticals
We could call the new miracle drugs "Socrac" and "Hypac"
and combine these with counselling and support

If this fails we could say a prayer:
O Socrates, O Great Thinker, O Great Questioner
O Challenger of the Youth, we beg you to reincarnate
We will provide you with the best educators and counsellors

Or we could forego scientific and religious zeal
and require critical thinking courses from kindergarten through
   to Ph.D.
teaching each human to think

President's Inauguration: The Man

His eyes did not light up like rockets and take off
before the massive crowd zooming around in a flashy display
His heart did not break out of his chest
and show itself to be ten times the normal size
His speech was not in twenty different languages at once
   promising peace
His energy was not equal to or more than
the energy of the billions listening to him with worship in their eyes
His shoulders did not bulge like the Incredible Hulk's
to carry the world's full weight
He did not introduce an invention of warp time travel
   or time machines
He did not fly

Mother's Day

I wanted to send my mother flowers
on this day
but this would have been like sending
flowers to my grave

I wanted to talk to her
have conversations
but she always preferred me
silent, stillborn

Now I wish all the flowers
that were never sent, killed in conception
could find a way to claw out from
beneath the ground

and unite us
in a powerful bouquet
a testament to the mother-daughter bond
incapable of defeat

so we too could participate in this
matriarchal festivity
take our seats in an ancient circle of stones

A Bouquet for My Mother from Vandussen Gardens

I choose the most exotic garden and walk around it slowly
collecting a bouquet of flowers for my mother:

some pink streaked yellow tulips
some Japanese water irises
some pink-white flowers from the umbrella plant
some feather grass to put in between
some fuchsia-purple flowers from the longleaf lungwort
some tall slim fuchsia bulbs from the Korean mint plant
some sky blue flowers from the Siberian bugloss
some orange Icelandic poppies
some bleeding hearts (paler than the ones in my mother's own garden)
some yellow-orange-red tupa flowers from the bell flower family
some more pink streaked yellow tulips
some dark purple pansies
some purple tulips with edges like the edges of cloth cut with
    pinking shears (looking like something my mother showed me
    how to make as an arts and craft)
daisies (looking as if they were made of shreds of plastic, like another
    thing she showed me how to make)
some elephant ears from the Saxifrage family (to support my mother
    in listening to all the music she enjoys)

I bless the bouquet with a splash of water from the garden fountain,
washing away all bitterness and hurt
then drop a penny in the pond hoping she receives this good wish gift

Mary Daly

Mary Daly
a triple goddess
poet, philosopher, theologian
She was a big sinner
matriarchal anti-pope
She didn't allow men to take
one of her classes
wanted to nurture women
and authentic discussion
I was one of her students
who she anointed as woman divine
gave me a lavender collar
my own small congregation
lavender prayer beads
She said they would foster
visionary imagination
She taught me about female prayer:
put your palms together
and curve your hands and fingers
to form the shape of a womb

She said every inch of a woman's body is clean
especially there
I had never heard that before
felt a heavy red cloud lift from below

*I met Mary Daly briefly in Boston during a conference on feminist philosophy. The poem should be taken on a metaphorical level. I wasn't literally her student, and she never literally taught me about female prayer. Her books touched me deeply on a personal level, and directed me to mentor and help empower other women.

portable shrine

meditating with prayer beads
at each stone I say a prayer
to spirits of the east, to spirits of the southeast
to spirits of the south, to spirits of the southwest
to spirits of the west, to spirits of the northwest
and to spirits of the north
completing an ancient circle of stones

*Since ancient times, many cultures have believed that stones from the earth possess unique
subtle energy. Prayer beads are a meditative device used in many religious faiths. Some
say ancient circles of stones were a form of amulet or talisman with healing powers and
that they could also have been used for ceremonial purposes.*

Sufi Heat Rose

sufi heat rose

my heart pressed against
his hers ours

*Sufis make this formation by holding hands and coiling into a tighter and tighter circle so that there are three or four close layers of people arm-in-arm, chest-to-back, head-to-shoulder; thus I have titled the poem "sufi heat rose."

male alto

enters the stage casually, humbly
an ageless genderless voice
mixes with other voices easily, attentively
his turn to strut
a full plumage of blues and greens
polyamorous awakening
love radiating from each peacock eye
teaches us, sacred lover

man who loves the lute

man who loves the lute
his wife and two small children
cares for his children
while his wife studies
after his performance he holds
the lute's full belly in front of his body
standing still, the rose
shoulder strap showing
honouring his beloveds

harpsichord

inside the winged-shaped instrument
a painting of naked cherubs
bathing, in the trees fluttering
their wings, one with a kitten
another with two rabbits
a plucking of golden strings
far removed from sinister sounds
the music of their safe playing
a children's heaven

mandala

we sang to each other
that we were each the goddess
and each the mother
struck ecstatic postures
arms above heads, around round bellies
turned and blessed each other
from roots to sky
formed sacred triangles in groups of three
shifted into circles
our different shapes, colours, spirits
moving north, south, east, west
made our own mandala

Acknowledgements

I am grateful to the editors of the journals and anthologies where some of the poems have appeared or will be appearing. I am also grateful to Andrea O'Reilly, founder and editor-in-chief of Demeter Press, for taking on and overseeing the book's publication. The book couldn't have had a better midwife. Finally, I owe thanks to Mary Saracino for her close reading of a final version of the manuscript and to Julie Hammond for her beautiful artwork for the cover.

"Young Nature Goddess" appeared in *Trivia Voices*.

"Endangered" appeared in *The Goose*.

"Siamese Cat" and "Feline Love" appeared in *The Brock Review*.

"homeless neighbour" appeared in *Magnolia: A Journal of Women's Literature*, Volume II, guest editor Karen Connelly.

"River" appeared in *Women and Environments*.

"Hospital Birth Record," "Alignment," "Mood Lenses," "Psychiatric Protocol," "Foot Poems," "Blue Eyes," "rage," "red dragonfly," and "Twins"—are presented in an artist's statement/theoretical commentary in "Psychological Disability, Poetry, and Aesthetic Values" in *Different Art: New Essays on Disability and Arts* edited by Christopher Smit and Raphael Raphael, Intellect Ltd., forthcoming.

"Vagina Dentata" appeared in *She is Everywhere*, Volume III, edited by Mary Saracino and Mary Beth Moser.

"On Reviving Socrates" appeared in *Philosophy Now*.

"mandala" appeared in *Ochre: Journal of Women's Spirituality*.

Andrea Nicki was born and grew up in Fredericton, New Brunswick. She has a Ph.D. in philosophy from Queen's University and held a postdoctoral fellowship at the Center for Bioethics at the University of Minnesota. Her first poetry book, *Welcoming*, was published by Inanna Publications in 2009. Her poems have appeared or are forthcoming in Canadian and international journals and anthologies such as *The Brock Review, Rampike, The Goose, Philosophy Now, Magnolia: A Journal of Women's Literature II, Women Write Their Bodies: Stories of Illness and Healing, My Body, My Health: Women's Stories, Different Art: An Anthology on Disability and Arts, Women and Environments International,* and *She is Everywhere: Volume 3.* She is Faculty Lecturer in narrative medicine and applied health ethics in the Department of Health Sciences at Simon Fraser University. She serves as a mentor for the SFU student health ethics club, and was the recipient of the Undergraduate Teaching Excellence Award in Health Sciences for 2011-2012.